KITCHEN

A Visual Library

TINA SKINNER

Schiffer Publishing Ltd

4880 Lower Valley Road, Atglen, PA 19310 USA

Copyright © 2002 by Schiffer Publishing Ltd.
Library of Congress Control Number: 2001095052

Designed by Bonnie M. Hensley
Cover design by Bruce M. Waters
Type set in LibertyD/ Korinna BT

ISBN: 0-7643-1510-2
Printed in China

Published by Schiffer Publishing Ltd.
4880 Lower Valley Road
Atglen, PA 19310
Phone: (610) 593-1777; Fax: (610) 593-2002
E-mail: Schifferbk@aol.com
Please visit our web site catalog at **www.schifferbooks.com**
We are always looking for people to write books on new and
related subjects. If you have an idea for a book please
contact us at the above address.

This book may be purchased from the publisher.
Include $3.95 for shipping.
Please try your bookstore first.
You may write for a free catalog.

In Europe, Schiffer books are distributed by
Bushwood Books
6 Marksbury Ave.
Kew Gardens
Surrey TW9 4JF England
Phone: 44 (0) 20 8392-8585;
Fax: 44 (0) 20 8392-9876
E-mail: Bushwd@aol.com
Free postage in the U.K., Europe; air mail at cost.

Courtesy of Bis Bis Imports Boston

CONTENTS

INTRODUCTION

Courtesy of DuPont

I started out this book with the best intentions to creating a visual sourcebook for the tiniest of kitchens, but...

As you'll see, it's hard to say no to big, to fancy, to stylish. Still, I tried to keep the criteria to "modest in scale," and when the pictures were just too good to turn away, I qualified this by adding "especially considering today's new housing." Nonetheless, most of us, as we shop for decorating and design ideas, are looking for ways to adapt what we see to what we have. We have a floor plan already in our existing home, or the architect's drawing. Opportunities may exist to remove a wall, incorporate a pantry or laundry room, or even bump the outside wall to create more room.

The ultimate goal, of course, is to personalize your space, to make it work with your family routine, and to create a place where you feel proud and at home.

This compendium of wonderful images will help you shop for colors, textures, and layouts that appeal to the way you live. Here is a chance to study cabinet doors, appliance colors and placement, flooring, wall color, and collection displays. Draw together your favorite elements to create the kitchen of your dreams. If you are shopping for a kitchen design professional, be sure to inquire at the National Kitchen and Bath Association. Their website, www.nkba.org, has all kinds of great tips for homeowners, and they will steer you toward a certified professional in your area when you're ready to get to work. Also, be sure to check out the resource guide at the back of this book if you want more information about dealership locations or designers who can help you get started.

Covenant Kitchens & Baths, Inc.

Chapter 1

COOK'S NOOKS

Kitchens are, bottom line, where the food is prepared. Perhaps the cook wants to invite visitors or helpers in, or to sit down with them in the kitchen after the work is done. These kitchens are all about the business and art of getting meals ready for the table. They're culinary offices, centers, or stages where a household's nourishment is artfully, efficiently, or, most of all, lovingly prepared.

When your kitchen is small, your cabinets end up packed. So showcase cabinetry benefits from curtains, which conceal while adding flair. The refrigerator and microwave, the two most-used appliances, were set outside of the cook's arena to increase access for the rest of the household. *Courtesy of Aristokraft®*

Bright white illuminates a small space. Here, even the largest appliance is accommodated in this small galley kitchen. *Courtesy of DuPont*

Eye-catching design accents show up all over this big city kitchen, from the checkerboard wallpaper to the cooking-inspired tiles set above the range. A large window covering most of one wall visually expands the room. *Courtesy of Wood-Mode Custom Cabinetry*

A cozy look was achieved for this apartment-sized kitchen through the use of faux brick wall treatment and rustic wood accents. Glass shelving over the sink adds an airy look to the room and, tucked underneath one of the cabinets, is a compact, built-in microwave. *Courtesy of Wood-Mode Custom Cabinetry*

Space was precious, but so are the owner's hands, so a dishwasher was a must. Here a compact unit is concealed under the sink. A nearby eating counter is also the kitchen's workspace. Efficiency is crucial. *Courtesy of Bis Bis Imports Boston*

Rich wood tones contrast with ImperiaSteel doors in this contemporary kitchen. Granite counters complete the look. *Courtesy of Imperia Corporation*

Despite its narrow shape, this kitchen is far from confining – thanks to the ten-foot ceiling and a half-wall constructed on one side. *Courtesy of Portland Cement Association*

In a "Zen Loft" he created for the Kohler Design Center, Canadian interior designer Brian Gluckstein melded rich mocha-finish cabinetry, Asian touches, industrial sleekness, and retro influences. Key ingredients in this modestly proportioned kitchen include multi-task activity centers. The marble island serves as working counter and water source, with a flip-up stainless steel countertop to provide additional space. *Courtesy of Kohler Co.*

Acrylic or glass block makes a sanitary backsplash above countertop, and allows natural light to flood areas that overhead lighting often misses. *Courtesy of Hy-Lite Products, Inc.*

11

Though modest in size, this remodeled circa 1840s farmhouse kitchen was designed to maximize both efficiency and charm. The sink, stove, and refrigerator are but a couple of steps away from the granite-topped island with seating for two. The designer also incorporated antique stained glass panels in the cabinet doors and made sure there was plenty of room to display the homeowners' collection of copper teakettles. *Courtesy of Wood-Mode Custom Cabinetry*

By adding floor to ceiling cabinets, the owners maximized their cupboard storage space and preserved countertop work area all the way around this small kitchen. A recessed ceiling adds height and air to the small room. *Courtesy of StarMark Cabinetry*

Below: This small New York City kitchen was updated with new high gloss laminate cabinets, black appliances, and black granite countertops, creating a beautiful and elegant contrast that can be seen from both the living and dining areas. A cantilever top extending to the dining room offers more seating options for the family. To achieve a uniform, streamlined look, architect Victoria Benatar Urban provided the refrigerator with custom panels in the same laminate. *Courtesy of Victoria Benatar Urban*

otography by David Taylor/Stylist: Raul Flores

Photography by David Taylor/Stylist: Raul Flores

A partition wall was eliminated and replaced with an island in this New York City apartment. Light birch cabinets below a gray stone countertop combine with glass fronted cabinets to achieve an airy, sophisticated look. *Courtesy of Victoria Benatar Urban*

The original cabinets in this narrow Manhattan kitchen did not meet the ceiling, creating underutilized space in an already tight area. To create more space and a cleaner look, architect Victoria Benatar Urban added a 12" laminated piece along the top cabinet to raise the storage space to the ceiling. Greater sophistication was achieved by replacing the laminated countertop with one of stainless steel and adding additional stainless steel details like a small shelf by the windowsill, radiator cover, and pull handles on the maple cabinets. High gloss decorator's white paint on the walls takes advantage of the reflective qualities inherent in the stainless steel. *Courtesy of Victoria Benatar Urban*

Photography by David Taylor/Stylist: Raul Flores

A once small, dark kitchen with a separate laundry area was redesigned to form this new space. A wall was cut back to allow for the new design, incorporating the laundry room with built-in washer and dryer plus a wraparound counter. The new opened space, measuring 10-1/2 x 14 feet, allowed for this peninsula, packed with storage on both sides, with a practical, all-purpose sink in the laundry area. *Courtesy of DRS and Associates*

A countertop arm extends from the wall at an angle. This allows two people access to the counter space and sink, narrowing down to the stove where only one person can (and should) work at a time. Oven, refrigerator, and additional cabinet storage space extend on into the dining area. *Courtesy of Distinctive Kitchen & Bath Interiors*

The owner of this approximately twelve foot by twelve foot kitchen undertook a complete remodeling job himself in order to update the circa 1960s painted oak cabinets and gain additional floor and counter space. A wall between the kitchen and dining room was removed, as were a small walk-in pantry and a bank of cabinets that originally housed a wall oven. The result was an open and airy floor plan, nearly double the cabinet storage area, and tons of additional counter space. Sleek brushed aluminum pulls on natural maple cabinets promote a classically modern theme that helps unify the stainless steel appliances and full-height backsplash. Black mica countertops banded on the edges in maple continue the theme and a vinyl floor in faux black and white marble provides added flair. *Courtesy of James F. Ruppel*

Stainless steel and a bold green work together for dramatic effect. Slashes of wood and steel shelving add to the modern look. *Courtesy of KitchenAid*

hoto by Mike Teipen

It's all in there, hidden by separate cabinet workstations that conceal dishwasher, microwave, conventional oven, and refrigerator. The ceramic stovetop was chosen to help blend in with black countertop. The floor print of the kitchen is only 9 by 11 feet, but enjoys enormous surroundings in what was once a big sunroom. *Courtesy of YesterTec*

A small kitchen offers big effect, with an impressive, wrap-around island rich with decorative molding. *Courtesy of Congoleum Corp.*

This room would once have been advertised as a kitchenette. Acrylic blocks installed above the windows add stature to the room, and accommodate a dark paint color on the walls that would have been stifling without the open wall. *Courtesy of Hy-Lite Products, Inc.*

Maple wood was given a mocha glaze over a natural finish for this glowing effect. A movable island has been pushed out to accommodate a second cook, and the rest of the family is welcome to pull up a stool at the counter. *Courtesy of Yorktowne Cabinets*

m Livingston, CKD

Custom designed tile work above the range highlights this cheerful kitchen, which also features two-tone cabinetry and marble insets at either end of a spacious island. *Courtesy of Wood-Mode Custom Cabinetry*

An undulating, mosaic backsplash provides visual contrast with the linear floor and cabinet pulls in this contemporary kitchen. Designer Jacqueline Mead saved counter space by incorporating a built-in microwave below the range. *Courtesy of Crystal Cabinet Works, Inc.*

Photography by Bruce Glass

This large island could easily have overpowered the room, so designer Brad Fortune finished it in rich black hues that blend seamlessly with the gray slate floor. He used black as well for the marvelous arched hood over the range and for handy open shelving just below, here filled with a collection of baskets. *Courtesy of Crystal Cabinet Works, Inc.*

Chapter 2
CORNERED

In a kitchen-slash-dining room, or a home with an open floor plan, the actual kitchen is often relegated to a corner. Here are images to prove that it is all you really need for a wonderful, functional kitchen.

Kitchen space in a Boston condo was at a premium in this remodeling project, so a chunk was taken out of the breakfast nook and a small dining counter added overlooking the cooking area. Blue lacquered cabinets and stainless steel appliances give this room its cool glow. *Courtesy of Interni/ABODE*

Nostalgia blends with modernism in a kitchen that makes maximum use of wall space. There's no chance of bumping your head on a cabinet door here, as the curved upper wall units open up and out of the way via a pneumatic piston lift door system. A corner element at the center of the lacquered workspace incorporates a built-in knife holder, pullout chopping board, utensil bar, and spice cabinets on either side. Cooks who aren't especially neat will appreciate the anti-drip edge countertops made of cherry laminate. *Courtesy of Snaidero USA*

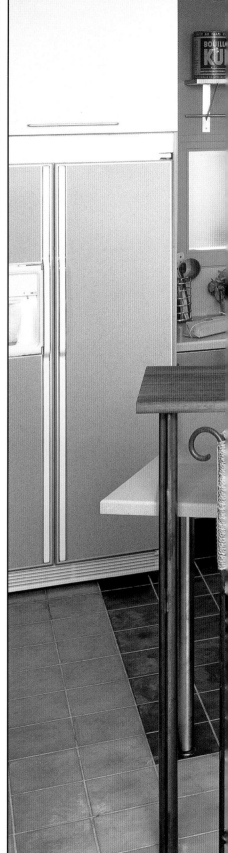

A raised eating counter creates exciting angles in three-dimensional, monochromatic space. Stacked cabinets accommodate an oven and provide extra storage space, while more cabinets are contained beneath a clean sweep of steely gray Corian® countertops.*Courtesy of DuPont*

The owners of this inviting kitchen borrowed space from a former porch area and powder room to create more room for casual entertaining as well as everyday living. Designed in a turn-of-the-century style, the kitchen features a wonderful expanse of ivory countertop, extra-large stainless steel stove, custom designed hood with brass and chrome tile liners, and a small television positioned directly across from the eating bar. Warm oak flooring sets off the eggshell cabinetry, which was extended over the countertop area for even greater storage space. *Courtesy of Wood-Mode Custom Cabinetry*

Cathy Larsen Jepson, CKD, CBD

Susan Larsen, CKD, CBD

27

A decorative display cabinet over the sink becomes a focal point for this windowless corner kitchen. Crisp white appliances and countertop blend with the wall coloring, allowing the woodwork to shine. *Courtesy of StarMark Cabinetry*

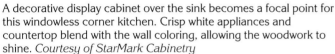

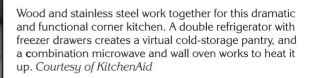

An island has been shifted right to give you greater insight into this kitchen, where stainless steel appliances are tucked beneath a black counter, and balanced by warm wood tones. *Courtesy of KitchenAid*

Wood and stainless steel work together for this dramatic and functional corner kitchen. A double refrigerator with freezer drawers creates a virtual cold-storage pantry, and a combination microwave and wall oven works to heat it up. *Courtesy of KitchenAid*

Above: A V-shaped kitchen is designed to maximize the tropical views in this Florida island home. The countertop is a combination of stainless steel and African Wenge wood. The lacquered, solid-panel cabinetry changes color to reflect different times of day and seasons in hues ranging from a plum cast to a blue, cocoa, or silvery gray. *Courtesy of Interni/ABODE*

Left: A bold choice of eggplant purple makes this kitchen unique and exotic. The color creates a decorative tile touch in the range hood, and a wonderful horizon line between the rich wood finish on upper and lower cabinets. *Courtesy of Yorktowne Cabinets*

Top right: A pretty white kitchen creates the perfect stage for a sociable chef. Recessed ceiling lights create even lighting, and black appliances add punctuation to large stretches of like-colored cabinetry. *Courtesy of KitchenAid*

Bottom center: Detailing in the cabinetry adds beauty to this kitchen – a darker stain in the lower panels, glass panes in the wall cabinets. Stainless steel appliances reflect the glow of the wood. *Courtesy of KitchenAid*

The sink was recessed into the corner, allowing someone to move in closer and use a space often wasted when it comes to utilit A lazy Susan in the cabinet above has a rim to keep items from falling on the person below. The addition of recessed shelving in combination with door racks enables you to see everything, without having to dig through to the items at the back. Hand-carved moldings add panache. *Courtesy of Wood-Mode Custom Cabinetry*

The glossy black farmer's sink provides a dramatic focal point for this country inspired kitchen, where old and new looks coordinate effortlessly. Designer Brad Fortune accented distressed pine cabinets with black granite countertops to blend with the sink. *Courtesy of Crystal Cabinet Works, Inc.*

Decorative details in the cabinetry give this room its charm. Interestingly, open display space was placed in lower cabinets for a cook who prefers to reach up for the everyday items. *Courtesy of Yorktowne Cabinets*

White cabinetry and appliances form a bright canvas for a great collection of kitchen antiques and accessories. The picture is underlined in resilient sheet flooring that picks up the copper tones in the hanging cookware. *Courtesy of Congoleum Corp.*

Workspace next to the range is enhanced with the addition of a semicircular extension to the countertop. Streamlined, red oak cabinetry lines the walls while walnut flooring and a paneled ceiling add warmth to this family oriented kitchen.
Courtesy of the Hardwood Council

This is typical of the older kitchen – a long, hall-like room. When remodeling this one, white cabinets were used to brighten up the space, contrasted with hunter green walls to highlight the space below the ceiling and make the room seem taller. *Courtesy of Kraftmaid Cabinetry*

Opposite page, top right: As sleek and chic as a racing car, this is a kitchen that defies convention. Its bold design consists of an unbroken unit of curvaceous workspace, finished in fiery red lacquer with a recessed gray base. Between the two layers of glossy red lies abundant room for kitchen essentials and accoutrements. *Courtesy of Snaidero USA*

This kitchen enjoys a cozy corner of the home, a corner stage where the cook can work while interacting with family members and guests beyond. The refrigerator has been concealed behind panels that match the cabinetry. *Courtesy of Distinctive Kitchen & Bath Interiors*

Center right: Nineteenth century charm combines with twenty-first century convenience in this uniquely styled kitchen. Fully functional, antique-look appliances are finished in glossy black enamel with satin brass trim and decorative scrollwork around the door castings. The six-burner range – with two smooth-top elements on the side, self-cleaning convection oven, and special food warmer unit – would be the envy of its Victorian ancestors. For large family meals or weekend entertaining, the homeowner can also use the built-in microwave or 3.8 cubic foot wall oven. *Courtesy of Elmira Stove Works*

Bottom right: A hearth-like area was created under the range, topped by a stainless-steel hood that works with the room's Asian feel. *Courtesy of KitchenAid*

37

Working within the confines of a narrow, small kitchen, designer Brian K. Fagan created a bank of off-white cabinetry along the outside wall to brighten the room. This allowed for the pizzazz of a brick surround for the range unit. A movable island divides the room and creates additional storage space and work area. Beyond, in the dining area, additional cabinetry creates a small office area as well as storage for additional food and tableware. *Courtesy of Distinctive Kitchen & Bath Interiors*

When a Manhattan hotel was converted into apartments, the resulting kitchens were so small they were virtually useless. To achieve a far more practical and spacious area, architect Victoria Benatar Urban removed a wall and integrated the kitchen directly into the dining area. Stainless steel appliances blend wonderfully with the cherry cabinets, granite countertop, and wood flooring, while rounded wooden shelves add a decorative touch to the existing water pipe by the sink. *Courtesy of Victoria Benatar Urban*

Photography by David Taylor/Stylist: Raul Flores

A big, granite-topped island becomes cooktop and tabletop for this impressive eat-in kitchen. Matching cabinetry conceals the refrigerator while allowing the icemaker to join in a display of sleek black appliances. *Courtesy of Fieldstone Cabinetry.*

Black appliances and countertop work with honeyed tones in wood and tile for a warm, inviting little kitchen. *Courtesy of StarMark Cabinetry*

A traditional kitchen lines up floor and wall cabinets, divided by a stretch of countertop workspace. *Courtesy of StarMark Cabinetry*

Opposite page, bottom: Lots of ligh and plenty of white make a small roor bright. *Courtesy of Aristokraft©*

There are a lot of advantages to small – a cook can really minimize her travel when everything is close at hand. The secret is to set the refrigerator outside the work area so thirsty friends and family can grab a drink without getting in the way. *Courtesy of Aristokraft®*

Chapter 3

A LONG STRETCH

Here are kitchens stretched out along one wall. This wonderful linear arrangement allows a homeowner to maintain a truly open floor plan, and to situate the kitchen as part of the larger home.

Sleek and modern, this home demanded its kitchen meet par. Aluminum and charcoal laminate finishes blend cool with warm, a blend that keeps this kitchen cozy while emphasizing functionality. *Courtesy of Varenna Poliform*

Left: A ray of sunshine yellow streaks across this kitchen, captured between panels of fresh white cabinetry. *Courtesy of Fieldstone Cabinetry*
Top right: Steel and natural cherry make bold slashes through this kitchen, built for both production and beauty. *Courtesy of Varenna Poliform*
*s***Bottom:** All the elements are lined up for a uniform surface. The steel backsplash and hoods underline the functionality of the kitchen, complemented by worktop in beech slats. *Courtesy of Varenna Poliform*

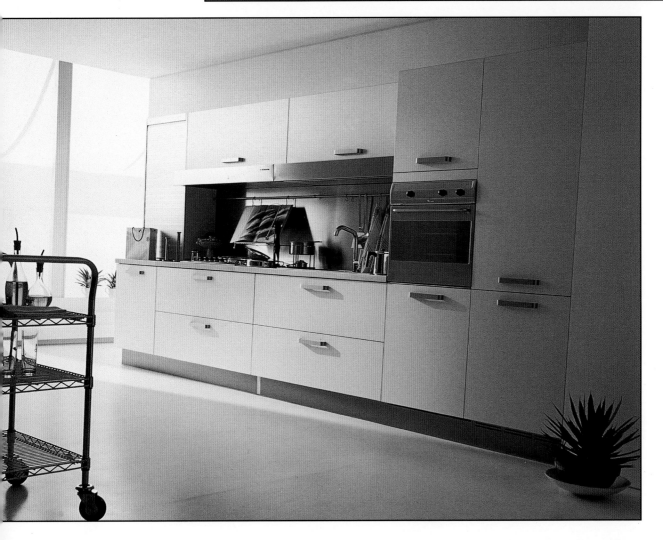

44

Interruptions in color create a more interesting space on a one-wall kitchen. Glass-fronted drawers offer tantalizing insight, yet enough obstruction to mar a messy view. *Courtesy of Varenna Poliform*

Opposite page
Top: A sophisticated, dramatic kitchen was inspired by the minimalist look, packed with high tech efficiency. Ergonomically designed, handle-free doors – finished here in cherry wood – are aesthetically pleasing and highly functional. *Courtesy of Snaidero USA*

Bottom: Simple and streamlined, this contemporary kitchen combines linen beige, pullout cabinetry below with interior-lit, satin glass panels above. The clean, white tile backsplash effortlessly ties the two together into a unified whole. *Courtesy of Snaidero USA*

Earth and sky are reflected in a black and white color theme, separated by a horizon of light. *Courtesy of Varenna Poliform*

There was very little space to work with in this Charlestown, Massachusetts, loft, so designer Henry L. Miller made the kitchen the focal point of the entire home. Surrounded by living room and dining room, the result is a place where guests can mill about but always see and take part in the action of the kitchen. The kitchen components are very industrial, with stainless steel, white Formica countertop edged in brushed aluminum trim, and white cabinetry with brushed aluminum hardware. *Courtesy of Interni/ABODE*

Opposite page, top: The look of weathered tile is captured in resilient sheet flooring for this handsome slash of kitchen with an elegant picture window. Pull up a seat for a view of the great outdoors in Asian-inspired dining chairs arranged at a tiled counter. *Courtesy of Congoleum Corp.*

Bottom left: A long rectangular kitchen was only partly separated from the dining room by the addition of a stylish glass panel. The two-level island is only a few steps away from the appliances lining both walls. *Courtesy of Portland Cement Association*

Bottom right: An experiment in the unusual, this stretch of countertop plays with shapes and touches of color, and luminous surfaces are accented by natural light. *Courtesy of DuPont*

A playful designer married red, white, and blue for this small cooking space. *Courtesy of Varenna Poliform*

Built-in cabinetry helps break up the straight line of a one-wall kitchen. *Courtesy of Diamond Cabinets*

The versatility of this kitchen is not immediately apparent. The cherry wood panel over the sink, however, is actually a folding door that can be opened from either side. Halogen lighting is incorporated into the fixed canopy atop the folding panel. The kitchen's uncluttered look is achieved through a minimum of cabinet hardware and a smooth cooktop with stainless steel backsplash. *Courtesy of Poggenpohl U.S., Inc*

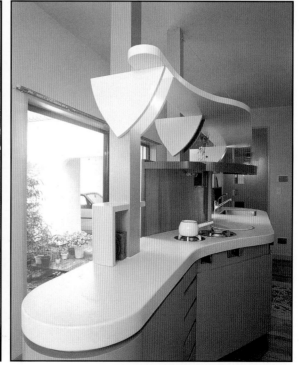

Chapter 4

WALK THROUGH KITCHENS

Sometimes a kitchen is a space on the way to another place. It's a wide hallway, where work gets done at mealtime.

Big windows open this kitchen to the great outdoors and provide lots of natural light, which is supplemented by halogen lighting subtly integrated under the sleek, satin-frosted wall units. Light maple veneer cabinetry is perfectly balanced by Belgian granite countertops and light slate ceramic flooring. *Courtesy of Poggenpohl U.S., Inc.*

Here the kitchen had to be stretched along one wall. The task was artfully accomplished, however, alternating stainless steel appliances and work areas with pantry-size cabinets. *Courtesy of KitchenAid*

Bottom right: Long, but far from narrow, this striking kitchen uses variations on the same design motif to achieve a pulled-together look. A metal grid inlaid onto the concrete floor is echoed by frosted panels at the top of the cabinetry and by the metal door pulls. Larger squares in the backsplash continue the theme. *Courtesy of Brookhaven Cabinetry*

Slate flooring and sunny yellow walls characterize this bright kitchen. Cheerful check chairs sit at either side of the cook's work area for a party atmosphere. *Courtesy of Kitchens Unique*

A kitchen in an old farmhouse feels bigger when the walls that separated a stairwell and a back hallway are removed. Though built to match the new cabinetry, the old hall wall is now graced with a ball-footed unit that looks like an antique, but is much more spacious than what grandma had. *Courtesy of Kraftmaid Cabinetry*

What was once an outside entry becomes a stylish if somewhat cramped kitchen. The most is made out of one wall for cabinetry and workspace, while allowing the unfinished brick wall and archway to shine. Cross-Colors® and water-jet technology create a traditional quilt pattern floor. *Courtesy of Crossville Porcelain Stone/USA*

53

Opposite a traditional U-shaped food preparation area stands a lovely built-in hutch finished in antique white. Designer Lynn Larson used distressed pine for the rest of this kitchen's cabinetry, including the large wet bar area tucked into a nearby niche. *Courtesy of Crystal Cabinet Works, Inc.*

Chapter 5

BARRIER REEFS

Here's a kitchen designed for the cook who likes plenty of company and plenty of sunshine! A wonderful center-arched window over the sink and a huge bay window in the dining area shower the room with natural light. Designer Brett Gonsalves included a large, two-level island with lots of corner shelving to display favorite possessions. The beaded maple cabinets are finished with warm brown highlights and feature custom designed crown moldings. *Courtesy of Crystal Cabinet Works, Inc.*

Opposite page, top: Bathed in light from an adjoining deck and huge arched windows, this kitchen was designed in beautiful shades of coffee and cream with aluminum accents. White laminate cabinetry is flanked by open shelving, adding to the airy feel of the room. Tucked into a corner till needed, the coordinated serving trolley is made of aluminum and solid beech and features adjustable shelving. *Courtesy of Poggenpohl U.S., Inc.*

Bottom: Step back in time to a charming country kitchen with contemporary conveniences. Kitchen essentials can be tucked away in the tall red oak cupboard or stored within easy reach on open shelving just above floor level. *Courtesy of Crystal Cabinet Works, Inc.*

This kitchen features a trio of striking wall units that open up and out to reveal tons of interior storage space. The backlit bottom doors are constructed of blue, satin-frosted glass with aluminum frames, while the top portions and matching cabinetry are done in warm chestnut. The center island boasts a cooktop and grill, with convenient open shelving underneath. *Courtesy of Poggenpohl U.S., Inc*

This high-tech, sophisticated kitchen includes ergonomically designed, handle-free doors finished in beige laminate. This kitchen is as aesthetically pleasing in its minimalist approach as it is highly functional. *Courtesy of Snaidero USA*

Floor-to-ceiling cabinetry creates the feeling of a warm, paneled room. *Courtesy of Yorktowne Cabinets*

Simple, sleek lines define the feel of this contemporary, Italian-inspired kitchen. Warm, cherry cabinets line two walls and the center island. Around the corner is a matching double-door pantry set slightly back to increase floor space. Distinctive features include a sensor-activated interior lighting system and practical white stone worktop on the island. *Courtesy of Snaidero USA*

Top: A galley kitchen becomes cook's delight when boundaries are extended into an adjoining room. A center island eating ba bridges the open area, and contemporary elements throughout form a cohesive space. *Courtesy of DuPont*

Bottom: A walkthrough kitchen uses black marble flooring and distinctive dark wallpaper to really make maple cabinetry pop. *Courtesy of Yorktowne Cabinets*

Left open the view, one wall is the focus of three rooms, each limited in space, and open to the others. The kitchen area is a compact U-shape. Repeating squares in the windows, cabinet doors, and tile countertops create an illusion of more space.
Courtesy of Weather Shield Windows & Doors

A wrap-around Corian® countertop provides both seating and workspace in this compact kitchen. Striking design elements include a copper range hood, bright red cabinetry, and stainless steel pole shelving system. *Courtesy of DuPont*

Sage green works with the natural finish on maple cabinetry for a cool country feel. This efficient kitchen is entirely self-contained, with plenty of space for the larder, along with bookshelves, built in breadbox, and decorative plate racks. *Courtesy of Yorktowne Cabinets*

Chapter 6

CENTRAL DIVIDE

Emerald tiles form frames for wood cabinetry, and contrast for the patterned white tiles on countertop and backsplash. *Courtesy of Bis Bis Imports Boston*

Ten foot ceilings add a feeling of spaciousness to this room, and two big floor-to-ceiling windows help add to the illusion of grand scale. Look, however, to the floor, where a central tile area breaks up the lines in a wood floor and supports a large, central island workstation. *Courtesy of Merillat Industries*

This beautiful kitchen combines classic, serene styling with cutting edge functionality and convenience. For maximum durability and resilience, an innovative poly-resin based material was used for both the countertops and sink basins. Italian designer Massimo Iosa Ghini incorporated an attractive and wonderfully versatile central island that includes a bottle rack, large wooden pastry board, multipurpose divided drawers, and overhead soffit for hanging utensils. Large pantry cabinets of varying heights surround double wall ovens. *Courtesy of Snaidero USA*

The straight and simple lines of sleek, modern cabinetry add elegance to intensive storage space. The wooden floor, crafted from narrow boards, helps add the illusion of width to this room. *Courtesy of Distinctive Kitchen & Bath Interiors*

A wood-lover's kitchen, the warm tones of this room extend beyond the house to the fence beyond. *Courtesy of Diamond Cabinets*

Dark cabinetry directs traffic in a small kitchen while giving the room its stately air. *Courtesy of Fieldstone Cabinetry*

Lighted display cabinets and architectural accents create a classic kitchen design. The arch shape over range and plate rack is mirrored in the island countertop. *Courtesy of Wellborn Cabinet, Inc.*

67

This farmhouse-inspired kitchen features floor to ceiling wall cabinets in an antique distressed red. The large center island is made of maple with a maize finish and doubles as a dining table. *Courtesy of Plain & Fancy Custom Cabinetry*

What looks like open shelving next to the refrigerator is actually a scrolling cabinet that retrieves items from above or below without making you stoop or stretch to fetch them. The system is button operated, and includes safety features that prevent smashed fingers or broken plates. *Courtesy of Kardex Systems, Inc.*

A central island greatly expands the workspace in this kitchen, and adds storage too. *Courtesy of Fieldstone Cabinetry*

Asia influenced this blend of beautiful maple and bird's eye maple woods, with black appliances and countertop. *Courtesy of Plain & Fancy Custom Cabinetry*

A checkerboard floor and backsplash add interest to a room rich in earth tones. *Courtesy of Schrock Cabinets*

Maple cabinetry complete with plate racks and curtained glass windows add elegance to this corner kitchen. *Courtesy of Schrock Cabinets*

Chapter 7

PULL UP A STOOL

A kitchen can be the most sociable room in the home. Here is where we gather for the morning ritual rush hour, filling our cereal bowls and coffee mugs to fuel up for the day. When it's over, the kitchen is where the day's events are discussed as dinner is prepared, or over a warm cup of tea or milk before bed.

Varied heights in the second tier of cabinets add interest to this stage-like kitchen, open on two sides to living and dining areas of the home. *Courtesy of Schrock Cabinets*

Photography by Lori Black

There's nothing ordinary about this kitchen, which features soothing green laminate cabinets topped by maple-framed doors. Designer Layne Cook incorporated a range and wet bar into the huge maple island, and added playful stools for a splash of color. *Courtesy of Crystal Cabinet Works, Inc.*

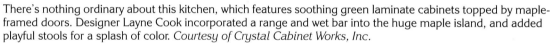

This French country style kitchen is a dream come true for wood lovers. Beautiful detailing adorns the maple cabinetry, which was finished with brown highlights. The room achieves greater visual depth by extending the window twelve inches out from the sink area. *Courtesy of Crystal Cabinet Works, Inc./Villa Kichenne*

This room is tonally rich, with metallic hues and wood tones forming a harmony accented by blue and green notes. *Courtesy of Kitchens Unique*

A handy seamstress has matched curtains to barstool covers, color-keyed to work with green laminate counters and a honeyed finish on lustrous wood cabinetry. *Courtesy of StarMark Cabinetry*

This household enjoys their morning news along with breakfast each morning, and they don't have to stray too far from the coffee pot. *Courtesy of StarMark Cabinetry*

A cook's sacred corner is marked off by a long swath of counter. Barstools beyond afford the chef company, as well as an audience. *Courtesy of StarMark Cabinetry*

Frills add thrills to this room – wrought iron stools, a two-tiered curved countertop, and a scalloped window treatment are hallmarks of this kitchen. State-of-the-art appliances, on the other hand, are demurely concealed behind wood panels that match the cabinetry. *Courtesy of KitchenAid*

Dark wood stain creates a rich first impression, underlined by patio-brick resilient sheet flooring. The designer completed the look with elegant details like the hanging lamp and decorative molding on the range hood. *Courtesy of Congoleum Corp.*

Tapered columns and a wrap-around counter separate kitchen from dining and living areas beyond. *Courtesy of Congoleum Corp.*

Designer Sharon Thomas employed different finishes on maple to create a delightful two-tone effect. The contrasting drawers, moldings, and cabinet panels were obtained with a cherry stain on the otherwise naturally finished maple. Ocean blue tile and chair seats add a dash of bright color. *Courtesy of Crystal Cabinet Works, Inc.*

A stately kitchen is achieved with crown molding on rich cherry cabinets. Designer Lynn Larsen used an inset beaded door style for added elegance and tucked a handy folding door niche into one corner. *Courtesy of Crystal Cabinet Works, Inc.*

White enamel finish on the cabinets is easy to maintain and gives this sunny kitchen a comfortable, casual feel. The designers added a copper hood and copper insets to the backsplash for a little extra pizzazz. *Courtesy of Crystal Cabinet Works, Inc./Metro Design*

Knocking down a wall and opening the kitchen to another living area is the most popular way of enlarging the food preparation space. Here additional cabinet space was added by adding a floor-to-ceiling unit that pans the cooking/dining area, as well as under-the-counter cabinets at the end of an island eating/food prep area. *Courtesy of Kraftmaid Cabinetry*

A lot of space was sacrificed for this handsome range hood – a sacrifice that was well worth it, and important to a homeowner who enjoys cooking on the stovetop. Walls were removed to open the kitchen to a dining area, but intimate space was maintained with a small seating area at the island. *Courtesy of Kraftmaid Cabinetry*

An island labors hard as both breakfast nook and work/clean-up station. Matching cabinetry conceals the side-by-side refrigerator and freezer unit and creates a floor-to-ceiling pantry, leaving room for decorative glass-front cabinets flanking the range hood. *Courtesy of Yorktowne Cabinets*

A copper range hood and staggered cabinets work together to create an interesting line and break up a square kitchen. *Courtesy of Yorktowne Cabinets*

Honeyed wood tones soften black granite and stainless steel in this kitchen, where old and modern meet.
Courtesy of Yorktowne Cabinets

With no walls to break up the kitchen and living areas, this home achieves a wonderfully spacious look, one worthy of its majestic floor to ceiling windows. The linear design of the windows is mirrored by a long row of side by side, glass fronted cabinets in the kitchen.
Courtesy of Portland Cement Association

A monochromatic color scheme defines the kitchen area and gives this room a fresh, airy appeal. Everything, from the cabinets to the cooktop to the television set, benefits from the creamy white hue. A beautiful hardwood floor and oak dining set provide just the right amount of contrast. *Courtesy of Portland Cement Association*

This small kitchen is packed with warmth and charm. Two contrasting cabinet finishes – a natural stain and a rich green work with plaid wallpaper create visual interest. Molding accents add depth. *Courtesy of Kraftmaid Cabinetry*

Chapter 8

EAT-IN KITCHENS

The family often gathers in the kitchen to eat, reserving the dining room (if there is one) for more formal occasions.

Opposite page, top: Two arches flank an open kitchen and dining area, bridged by a wall-length wooden shelf stained to match the cabinetry below. *Courtesy of Bis Bis Imports Boston*

Below: Small in size, this eat-in kitchen makes a big impression. Radiating roof beams, an arched entry to a patio room, and inset workstations are unique architectural elements. *Courtesy of Bis Bis Imports Boston*

All curves and contours, glossy cabinets hug the wall and flow easily into an oblong eating or serving bar just behind the range. Marbleized granite countertops and matching backsplash continue the unbroken, state-of-the-art look. *Courtesy of Snaidero USA*

Sunny yellow and white work to brightly define work and display areas. Stainless steel appliances add to the illumination. *Courtesy of KitchenAid*

Opposite page, top: This kitchen is open to the bright sunroom beyond. The island also functions as dinner table for the family. *Courtesy of Distinctive Kitchen & Bath Interiors*

Who wouldn't sacrifice storage space for a view like this? Still, room was found along the wall of cabinetry for a decorative plate rack and a basket bin. *Courtesy of Simonton Windows*

Opposite page, bottom: Dramatic red laminate cabinetry contrasts with stainless steel appliances in this stylish, futuristic kitchen. *Courtesy of KitchenAid*

A bench seat in the window is a wonderful space-saver, and an inviting place to linger. Stripes in the textiles imitate the plate rack. *Courtesy of Congoleum Corp.*

Cheerful blues and golds punctuate a clean, bright kitchen, home to a tea lover and a perfect place to share a cup along with the latest juicy gossip. *Courtesy of Yorktowne Cabinets*

Old-fashioned appeal was built in to this wonderful log cabin-style kitchen, with two tones of cabinetry to create the feeling of antique furnishings. *Courtesy of Plain & Fancy Custom Cabinetry*

This cheerful kitchen features a sunny breakfast nook tucked into a generous bay window. Cottage inspired cabinets topped by matching cream tiled countertops flank the generously sized, stainless steel appliances. Custom tiles behind the cooktop and in the glass cabinets on either side of the hood provide additional flair. A limestone-top island houses drawers on two sides plus an old-fashioned library display for cookbooks, with space left over for additional storage. A beautiful as well as practical piece of furniture, the island has electrical outlets on two sides and is designed so that the electric source is not visible. The bricks on the floor are one hundred years old, recycled from France. *Courtesy of Cross Interiors*

Space saving is one thing, time saving another. This rapid-cook
freestanding range cooks twice as fast using a combination of
radiant heat and microwave energy; and it requires no preheating.
Courtesy of Maytag Appliances

Green accents highlight a clean, white kitchen. The eat-in island table/work station also incorporates storage and display space. *Courtesy of Yorktowne Cabinets*

A kitchen area is often part of a larger, great room in today's new houses. Boundaries are defined by islands, leaving visual access to the rest of the "room." *Courtesy of Yorktowne Cabinets*

A stone-encased woodstove takes center stage in this camp kitchen, where rugged meets refined. Around the corner, a built in bar and wine rack also doubles as larder for dry goods and specialty oils and vinegars. *Courtesy of Plain & Fancy Custom Cabinetry*

Inset stripes in the flooring make this kitchen more negotiable for the sight impaired. Likewise, white porcelain knobs on natural wood cabinetry are visual cues. *Courtesy of Diamond Cabinets*

A small island is better than no island at all. Here it is moveable, so it can be shifted out toward the eating area, or in when the space beyond is needed. A railing above the cabinetry creates a decorative area for special displays. *Courtesy of Diamond Cabinets*

Storage cabinets continue outside the kitchen area and into the dining room to help maximize space for food and serving dishes. Notice the shelf extending from the range hood – a handy area to keep cooking oils and seasonings. *Courtesy of Schrock Cabinets*

Turned legs under the sink and stovetop create the look of custom furniture, breaking up the long lines of matching cabinetry. *Courtesy of Wellborn Cabinet, Inc.*

Chapter 9

OPEN FLOOR PLAN

Above: A deep peninsula offers storage on either side. An illuminating backsplash, white gloss lacquer on the cabinetry, and aluminum and glass display cases create an otherworldly effect. *Courtesy of Varenna Poliform*

Left: A kitchen nook includes countertop seating for one helper, as well as a wonderful display cabinet complete with cup rack and spice drawers. Staggered cabinet heights add interest. *Courtesy of Yorktowne Cabinets*

Beyond the kitchen, a home office center has been set up in matching cabinetry. Spillover storage from the food-prep area can be kept here as well. *Courtesy of Yorktowne Cabinets*

Below: A drop ceiling unit with decorative molding sheds light on a two-tier island work station that houses sink, dishwasher, microwave, and storage space, and still manages to double as seating area. Two showcase cabinets and a beautiful hand-painted grapevine beyond frame a tiled hood vent. And the pantry is artfully arranged behind cabinet doors set flush with the wall. *Courtesy of Distinctive Kitchen & Bath Interiors*

Informality with flair defines the feel of this comfortable kitchen, made visually larger by opening directly into the family room. A built-in, corner alcove keeps the television accessible but out of the way, while pullout wicker baskets are an attractive storage option under the countertop. Warm ceramic tile on the floor and copper fixtures on the bow-shaped center island add to the relaxed atmosphere. *Courtesy of Hanford Cabinet and Woodworking*

Blue countertop and blue stripes set the friendly tone for this functional, white kitchen. A corner tambour houses a coffee making station, neatly tucked away after hours. *Courtesy of Yorktowne Cabinets*

Photography by Carl G. Saporiti

A brick red finish on the wood floor keys in with a genuine brick wall, cut to make room for a microwave oven. Crisp white cabinetry allows the homeowner broad license with the palette of display items, making for a cheerful, bright space. *Courtesy of StarMark Cabinetry*

Designer Helen Marshburn recreated the wonderful look of an old fashioned hearth on one wall of this comfortable kitchen. A striking copper backsplash, hardwood floor, and creamy stucco walls accent the cabinets, finished in bisque with brown highlights. *Courtesy of Crystal Cabinet Works, Inc.*

Small in terms of floor space, this room gets stature from exposed ceiling beams.
Courtesy of Yorktowne Cabinets

Photography by Batista/Moon

Opposite page

Top: A central cabinet is elevated over the range to break up the top line. Neutral tones blend together seamlessly from floor to ceiling, allowing for splashes of blue or any other color the homeowner might choose. *Courtesy of Congoleum Corp.*

Bottom left & bottom center: This kitchen in a charming beach cottage overlooking the Long Island Sound was designed to fit the casual lifestyle of summering at the shore. The center island with honed granite countertop is perfect for serving the "crew," while crisp blue and white tile and wood floors add to the beach look. Waterproof wood countertops wrap around a curved banquet, reminiscent of a classic yacht interior. *Covenant Kitchens & Baths, Inc.*

Left: With a distinctly southwestern look, this graceful kitchen features a beamed, cathedral ceiling, maple cabinetry, and warm ceramic floor with matching backsplash. Designer Kelly Wilson included a long, rectangular island with a double sink and plenty of workspace. *Courtesy of Crystal Cabinet Works, Inc.*

Below: Different drawers and doors on the cabinets add interest in this contemporary, open-floor-plan kitchen. *Courtesy of Schrock Cabinets*

Chapter 10

OFF THE WALLS

One of the simplest ways to set your kitchen apart from the rest is to put everything under the counter. This frees up the wall for art and displays, creating an open, airy atmosphere. Of course, you have to have a kitchen big enough to accommodate all your storage needs in this way.

Here's a throwback to our grandmother's kitchen, with the long farmer's sink, grand slabs of wood, and open shelving for storage. *Courtesy of Bis Bis Imports Boston*

Staining window frames and cabinets alike builds a seamless look. A built-in shelf flush with the window tops maximizes a small space for display. *Courtesy of Weather Shield Windows & Doors*

Two kitchens in one, space was created to accommodate multiple cooks in their tasks, as well as a shelf that extends for informal dining or additional work area. *Courtesy of Bis Bis Imports Boston*

A thick slab of rich wood overlays a sophisticated collection of cabinetry in tones of butter and cream. *Courtesy of Varenna Poliform*

Storage is below in this modular kitchen, with only a swath of frosted glass cabinetry on the walls for dramatic and functional effect. *Courtesy of Bis Bis Imports Boston*

A wall of glass cabinetry helps expand the space while filling it. *Courtesy of Varenna Poliform*

Stainless steel, concrete, and red laminate work together for a stunning style statement. This is a kitchen designed to draw admiration. *Courtesy of Get Real Surfaces*

Chic, high tech Italian design fits neatly into a cozy, compact kitchen built under a sloping roof. Cherry cabinets alternate with aluminum appliances and softly lit, satin glass panels, all complemented by light hardwood flooring and a butcher-block breakfast bar. For coffee fanatics, there's a wonderful built-in coffeemaker complete with handy drawer for beans, supplies and utensils.
Courtesy of Snaidero USA

Wood and natural stone elements are juxtaposed with stainless steel in this neo-classical kitchen design by Mary Douglas Drysdale of Washington, D.C. Hand-painting and stenciling on the Canac cabinets and a center island, a forged-iron pot rack, and a sunburst mirror are among the many details that set this kitchen apart from the ordinary. A coved ceiling adds extra dimension to the space. *Courtesy of Kohler Co.*

It looks like wood flooring, but it doesn't sound like it. This resilient sheet flooring blends with cabinetry and a moveable island workstation while offering easy clean-up and maintenance to a busy homeowner. *Courtesy of Congoleum Corp.*

A second refrigerator holds cold beverages, a perfect serve-yourself unit right next to guest seating at the counter. *Courtesy of KitchenAid*

Chapter 11

QUICK CHANGEOVERS

Wheels, modular furniture, and clever cabinetry allow these kitchens to transform in a jiff, adding eating or workspace, or tucking it away when not needed. This is a chapter chock full of ingenious inventions that can add space and utility to your small kitchen.

Mobile, stainless steel units roll under a stationary Corian® countertop and backsplash with a vivid splash of color in cobalt blue. *Courtesy of DuPont*

Klineberg Photography

This whole room was done in laminates, carried through the pear-wood color in the cabinets. To make the space look bigger, the tile backsplash was carried beyond the end of the cabinetry, arching into the next room. These tiles are of un-gauged slate to add depth to the appearance. Notice how narrow the kitchen is – only four and a half tiles between the cabinets. *Courtesy of Distinctive Kitchen & Bath Interiors*

Angular lines give this kitchen its modern edge. Smoke and charcoal colors work with aluminum and glass for cool sophistication. *Courtesy of Varenna Poliform*

A fabulous pottery collection is housed in this unique, brick-floored kitchen. *Courtesy of Bis Bis Imports Boston*

Three finishes, including a weathered Indian corn yellow, hark back to the old world in this Provence-inspired kitchen. A freestanding French monk's table was incorporated, and the whole kitchen paved with stone flooring. *Courtesy of Plain & Fancy Custom Cabinetry*

One solution to limited space is to keep things mobile. Put table and work stations on wheels so you can roll them out of the way when you're not working in the kitchen and use the space for something else (put your couch on wheels, too). Here, this city dweller chose a sleek look for a loft apartment, with appliances in smoky gray contrasted against white walls and glass shelves. *Courtesy of Viking Range Corporation*

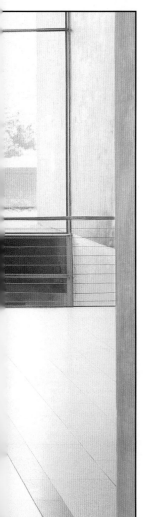

This streamlined kitchen is reminiscent of the 1960s, but reinterpreted for the twenty-first century. Stainless steel appliances are combined with high gloss laminate cabinetry featuring solid aluminum bar handles. The table and dual rolling cabinets underneath can be positioned wherever most practical to facilitate traffic flow through the kitchen. *Courtesy of Poggenpohl U.S., Inc.*

A wonderful space saver, this breakfast table slides out for a snack, and tucks away when the dishes are cleared. Japanese influence is apparent in frosted glass door panels resembling miniature shoji screens and in simplistic square cabinet knobs. *Courtesy of DuPont*

Faces can be deceiving. This kitchen contains a unit that looks like cabinet drawers, but which actually wheels out to act as a serving cart. Another pullout feature is a handy cutting board. *Courtesy of Wood-Mode Custom Cabinetry*

A bold backsplash color-keys with a moveable island worktable. Sunny yellow finishes on floor and cabinetry add to the happy atmosphere in this cozy kitchen. *Courtesy of Fieldstone Cabinetry*

A cleverly designed table wheels out for extra work or dining space when needed. *Courtesy of Wood-Mode Custom Cabinetry*

Floor space was maximized in this rotunda shaped kitchen designed by Stan Ward. An elegant rolling cart keeps essentials close by and a bi-level island provides plenty of seating space. Custom detailing on the cabinet moldings, hood rim, and island tie major elements of the room together. *Courtesy of Crystal Cabinet Works, Inc.*

Chapter 12

STORAGE AND RETRIEVAL

What it all comes down to in kitchens, basically, is appliances to do the work, and cabinetry to house the foodstuff, the implements, and the gadgets. The more places you have to tuck this stuff away, the more stuff you can have! And the neater your kitchen looks. Here's a look at some innovative systems for storing your stuff, and finding it again when you need it.

Floor-to-ceiling cabinetry maximizes the space in this relatively small kitchen. More storage was created by hanging cabinets over the island, which separates the kitchen from other areas in the house. Baking pans and dishes get their own slot in a special cabinet above double ovens. *Courtesy of Wood-Mode Custom Cabinetry*

An enormous amount of storage was built into this kitchen, behind handsome, rich blue doors that open to reveal shelves and drawers for storage. A bread bin and cutting board were tucked neatly under the counter. *Courtesy of Wood-Mode Custom Cabinetry*

Creamy white cabinetry was extended to an adjoining hallway to maximize storage space in this inviting kitchen. A convenient, built-in shelf over the range keeps spices and condiments within easy reach, while the large center island houses more cabinets under a cheerful blue/gray countertop. *Courtesy of Hanford Cabinet and Woodworking*

This space-effective kitchen blends with other areas of the home to create a warm, inviting gathering place for two or twenty. Abundant storage was built in to an entire wall of cabinetry that includes built-in double ovens. A seven-foot freestanding piece is a reservoir for a lifetime collection of cooking paraphernalia. And around the corner, in the mudroom, is a great wall of doors and drawers. *Courtesy of Plain & Fancy Custom Cabinetry*

This kitchen stretches along a hallway. The cabinetry was built with space saving features, like stacked lazy Susans in the corner cabinets and a mini pantry that utilizes the back of the door. *Courtesy of Plain & Fancy Custom Cabinetry*

Shiny blue adds bright background to glass and steel in this inviting modern kitchen. *Courtesy of Varenna Poliform*

An enormous window is left alone, with banks of storage on either side and work area in between. *Courtesy of Varenna Poliform*

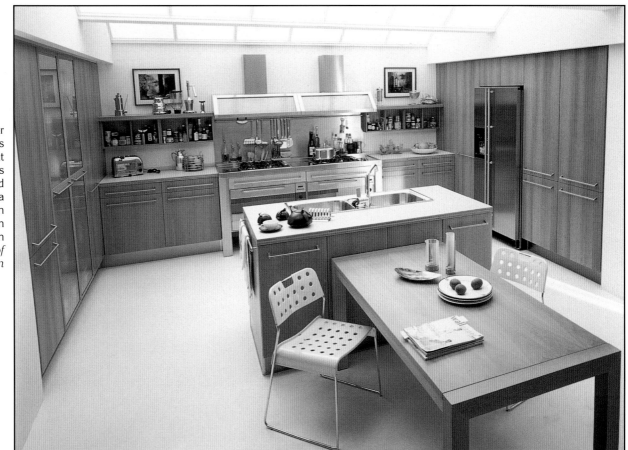

Created for cooking, this kitchen has great potential. It is as technical and functional as a professional kitchen while being as warm and cozy as a room can be. *Courtesy of Varenna Poliform*

By incorporating seating areas into a working island, the countertop space was doubled, and you still have an "eat-in" kitchen. *Courtesy of Kitchens Unique*

127

Artful design conceals clever ingenuity. A molded leg doubles as a pull to reveal a hidden spice rack. Handled baskets slide out, working as decorative and functional drawers. *Courtesy of Wood-Mode Custom Cabinetry*

Exciting design features set this kitchen apart, like the extended countertop with a semicircle ending shadowed above with wood and dramatic lighting. A stainless steel pole holds rotating shelves that keep condiments and spices close at hand. The central island with cooktop is elevated on a pedestal, giving the cabinetry a dramatic, floating effect. Besides beauty, this kitchen was designed for function. One cabinet is packed with wire racks that butterfly out, turning a small space into a virtual pantry where it is easy to find what you're looking for. A pullout knife rack creates a finger-safe storage unit for sharp blades. A lazy Susan in a corner unit allows you to store and access items all the way back. A stainless-steel bar and storage shelves create attractive displays for the everyday items of cooking, as well as a fold-down cookbook holder. *Courtesy of Brookhaven Cabinetry*

Keeping it simple and sleek – Shaker-style laminate cabinetry is gussied up with sunny wallpaper and a slash of blue countertop. Translucent rice paper and glass inserts on cabinet fronts add light and an illusion of space to floor-to-ceiling cabinetry. A tall pantry pullout creates convenient access to items stored in the backs of cabinets. Adjustable shelves let the food gatherer organize according to size and frequency of use. *Courtesy of Kraftmaid Cabinetry*

A pantry was created in cabinets against a far wall, with room for a bright wall of acrylic blocks for a mini greenhouse. *Courtesy of Hy-Lite Products, Inc.*

An Asian influence is felt in this room, where round and square forms contrast amidst straight, clean lines. *Courtesy of Hy-Lite Products, Inc.*

Wood and frosted glass create an Asian effect in this luxurious kitchen. An oversize drawer pulls out to reveal wire racks for well-lit storage. *Courtesy of Wood-Mode Custom Cabinetry*

Under all that majesty – a solid foot of crown molding – lies practical innovation. The coffee maker is concealed behind a swing-up panel, and below a lazy Susan helps pack a corner.
Courtesy of Wood-Mode Custom Cabinetry

The influence came from Asia, but the space-saving design is all-American. Cabinet doors have the shelves attached, so items swing out when you open, saving you from bending down and in to root around. A hinged shelf utilizes that tiny space in front of the sink, and becomes the perfect place to store those little essentials: scrubbies, hand lotion, and rubber gloves for messy jobs. Instead of a hinged door that opens to the trash bin, a drawer makes dropping messy things in much easier. This unit holds two tubs, to help you separate recyclables. *Courtesy of Wood-Mode Custom Cabinetry*

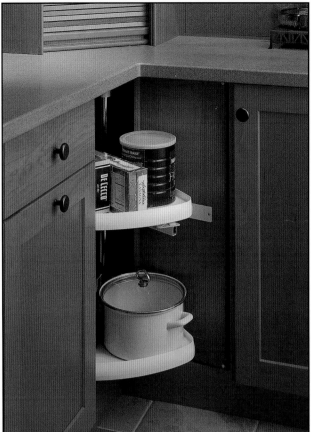

Designer Joyce Combs incorporated a medley of woods and textures into this kitchen, including tall cherry wall cabinets, beaded maple cabinetry in the cooking area, and an eye-catching mosaic countertop. A large country-style hutch on one wall was custom painted in sunny yellow. *Courtesy of Crystal Cabinet Works, Inc.*

Photography by Willie Gibsc

What could be more welcoming than a cozy fireplace right in the kitchen? This one is flanked by tall, slim windows that add visual height to the room. Directly in front is a square island with a convenient range and breakfast bar. Designer Ed Bader brought a classic country look to this kitchen with closed grain hardwood cabinets finished in white with brown highlights. *Courtesy of Crystal Cabinet Works, Inc.*

RESOURCE GUIDE

Aristokraft®
One Master Brand Cabinets Dr.
Jasper, IN 47546
812-482-2527
www.aristokraft.com
Aristokraft is a leading manufacturer of quality kitchen, bath, and home cabinetry. From the traditional beauty of oak to the radiant elegance of cherry, the company offers more than forty different styles and a multitude of accessories.

Bis Bis Imports Boston
4 Park Plaza
Boston, MA 02116
617-350-7565
www.bisbis.com
Bis Bis modular kitchens feature hand-painted ceramic tiles in large slabs for work areas, lava stone counters, and hand-carved marble sinks. Their island series accommodates the smallest spaces.

Brookhaven Cabinetry
One Second Street
Kreamer, PA 17833
800-635-7500
www.wood-mode.com
A companion line of Wood-Mode, Brookhaven provides semi-custom cabinetry in styles ranging from country to contemporary and traditional to high-tech. Their finishes provide an ideal blend of toughness and beauty.

Congoleum Corp.
Department C
P.O. Box 3127
Mercerville, NJ 08619-0127
800-274-3266
www.congoleum.com
One of the nation's leading manufacturers of resilient sheet and tile, resilient wood plank, and laminate flooring for more than one hundred years. All products are designed and manufactured in New Jersey, Pennsylvania, and Maryland.

Covenant Kitchens & Baths, Inc.
1871 Boston Post Road
Westbrook, Connecticut 06498
860-399-6241
Gerard Ciccarello, president of the firm, has been seen on the cover of Remodeling Magazine and his work has been published in national magazines, been awarded first place in NKBA design competition, and featured on Home and Garden Television.

Cross Interiors
6712 Colbath Avenue
Van Nuys, CA 91405
818-988-2047
cherylcaseyross@crossinteriors.com
www.crossinteriors.com

Cheryl Casey Ross is a Certified Interior Designer, a member of ASID, IIDA, and an AIA/SFV Professional Affiliate. She has clients all over the United States, has won numerous design awards, and has been published in over eighty books and magazines.

Crossville Porcelain Stone/USA
PO Box 1168
Crossville, TN 38557
931-484-2110
www.crossville-ceramics.com
Founded in 1986, this is the largest domestic manufacturer of porcelain stone tile for both residential and contract applications, and the exclusive distributor of Questech® Metals tiles and borders.

Crystal Cabinet Works, Inc.
1100 Crystal Drive
Princeton, MN 55371-3368
800-347-5045
763-389-5846
www.ccworks.com
Founded in 1947, this independent manufacturer produces custom cabinetry, handcrafted for long-lasting quality and beauty. Crystal specializes in finishes and design details, and the design flexibility to fit any lifestyle, from contemporary to country to traditional.

Decorá
One Master Brand Cabinets Dr.
Jasper, IN 47546
812-482-2527
www.aristokraft.com
For cabinetry that enhances the way you live, Decorá offers a variety of styles, finishes, and decorative elements to give you the freedom to create a personalized, elegant look for your home.

Diamond Cabinets
One Master Brand Cabinets Dr.
Jasper, IN 47546
812-482-2527
www.aristokraft.com
Style, quality, and choices ... Diamond provides quality cabinetry, offering current styles and popular storage and organization accessories for consumers who want to balance functionality, beauty, and price.

Distinctive Kitchen & Bath Interiors
5891 Firestone Drive
Syracuse, NY 13206
315-434-9011/Fax: 434-9013
www.idistinctiveinteriors.com
Design consultant Brian K. Fagan has been creating kitchen and bath designs for central New York clients since 1990. His designs have been featured in *Better Homes & Gardens* and in *Kitchens by Professional Designers*.

DRS and Associates
11684 Ventura Boulevard #861
Studio City, CA 91604

323-822-0123
www.drs-associates.com
DRS and Associates is a design firm specializing in the design and construction of upscale, quality kitchens and bathrooms. Services include general contracting, design consultation, project management, and remodeling/restoration of residential and commercial properties.

DuPont Corian®
P.O. Box 80012
Barley Mill Plaza — Building 12
Wilmington, DE 19880-0012
1-800-426-7426
www.corian.com
DuPont's Corian® surfaces offer timeless beauty and performance to suit a variety of design needs. Solid surfaces by Corian® help create warm, inviting rooms.

DuPont Zodiaq®
P.O. Box 80012
Barley Mill Plaza — Building 12
Wilmington, Delaware 19880-0016
1-877-229-3935
www.zodiaq.com
DuPont's Zodiaq® surfaces offer timeless beauty and performance to suit a variety of design needs. Zodiaq® quartz surfaces are just right for an elegant, contemporary look.

Elmira Stove Works
232 Arthur St. South
Elmira, Ontario, Canada N3B 2P2
800-295-8498
www.elmirastoveworks.com
Elmira's antique-styled appliance line includes ranges, convection wall ovens, microwaves, refrigerators and panel kits for refrigerators and dishwashers. These appliances add special warmth and character to any country, Victorian, or retro home.

Fieldstone, Inc.
600 E. 48th St. N.
Sioux Falls, SD 57104
605-335-8600
www.StarMarkCabinetry.com
Fine Fieldstone cabinetry offers choices to let you express yourself with full creative freedom. Choose from a comprehensive selection of woods, finishes, accessories, fashion elements, and true custom options.

Get Real Surfaces
37 West 20th Street Suite 304
New York, NY 10011
212-414-1620
Get Real Surfaces will create virtually anything that can be designed and made out of concrete, in any color. Product lines include kitchen countertops and vanities with integral sinks, floor material and tubs, tiles, fireplaces, and architectural details.

Hanford Cabinet & Woodworking
102 Ingham Hill Road
Old Saybrook, CT 06475
860-388-5055
www.hanfordcabinet.com
In business for two decades, Hanford is a custom design and fabrication firm specializing in high-end cabinetry for the home and office.

The Hardwood Council
P.O. Box 525
Oakmont, PA 15139
412-281-4980
www.hardwoodcouncil.com
The Hardwood Council produces free technical literature on working with North American hardwoods. Interior designers, architects, builders, and remodelers are invited to view and order the Council's literature on their website.

Hy-Lite Products, Inc.
101 California Avenue
Beaumont, CA 92223

1-800-827-3691
www.hy-lite.com
Acrylic block windows are about 70 percent lighter than glass, and Hy-Lite can custom make windows in almost any size and shape, and guarantee against cracking, flaking, chipping, or discoloration.
(kziprick@aol.com)

Imperia Corporation
343 Manley Street
West Bridgewater, MA 02379
508-894-3000
www.imperiacabinet.com
This company manufactures cabinets ranging in style from traditional wood with richly carved corbels, moldings, and furniture appointments to the high gloss, sleek feel of radius laminate doors.

Interni/ABODE
50 Terminal Street
Charlestown, MA 02129
617-242-4140
www.interniusa.com
This collaborative of architects and designers works closely with clients to successfully realize every project regardless of size. They consider monetary constraints, respect the need for value, and believe in the possibility to design without compromise.

Jim Bishop Cabinets, Inc.
P.O. Box 11424
Montgomery, AL 36111
800-410-2444, ext. 3017
www.jimbishopcabinets.com
Jim Bishop founded the company in 1964. Door styles are available in oak, maple, poplar, cherry, thermofoil, and melamine. Six standard finishes are offered as well as glazes, semi-opaque base coats, crackle, edge wear, and veiling.

Kardex Systems, Inc.
Post Office Box 171
Marietta, OH 45750
800-234-3654
www.kardex.com
Manufactures and distributes automated storage and retrieval systems for home and office. Their innovative kitchen design incorporates a vertical carrousel that mechanically presents items without forcing the homeowner to bend down or reach up.

KitchenAid
P.O. Box 218
St. Joseph, Michigan 49085
800-422-1230
www.KitchenAid.com
KitchenAid offers a full line of kitchen appliances, including dishwashers, cooktops, ovens, and refrigerators. The company also has a complete offering of portable appliances, including stand mixers, food processors, cutlery, cookware, and coffee makers.

Kitchens Unique
118 Depot Drive
Madison, MS 39110
601-898-1199/Fax: 898-1190
melkitch@kitchensunique.com
www.kitchensunique.com
Mellany C. Kitchens, CKD, began her own cabinet manufacturing facility in 1990. She specializes in kitchen design with emphasis on the high-end clientele. Past-president of her local NKBA chapter, she is current representative to the national organization.

Kohler Co.
Kohler, WI 53044
800-4-Kohler
www.kohler.com
Founded in 1873, it is one of the oldest and largest privately held companies in the United States. It markets its products under the brand names of Kohler, Sterling, Kallista, Ann Sacks, Robern, and Canac, and, in Europe, under Jacob Delafon, Neomediam, and Sanijura.

Kraftmaid Cabinetry, Inc.
15535 South State Avenue
Middlefield, Ohio 44062
440-632-2389
www.kraftmaid.com
The nation's largest built-to-order/semi-custom cabinetry manufacturer, KraftMaid's extensive product lines include more than 90 door styles in a variety of hardwoods and laminates.

Maytag Appliances
403 West Fourth Street North
Newton, IA 50208
888-462-9824
www.maytag.com
Since 1892, Maytag has manufactured appliances that provide dependability and innovation. Today, they continue a commitment to easing the work of life and enhancing the joy of living.

M.E. Tile Company, Inc.
6463 Waveland Ave.
Hammond, IN 46320
219-554-1877
www.metile.com
M. E. Tile Company, Inc. produces handmade, sculptured, low relief, ceramic tile suitable for kitchens, bathrooms, foyers, fireplaces, door and window frames. Over 500 raised relief single tile moldings, liners, mural, linear arrays, and arches are available.

Merillat Industries
5353 West U.S. Highway 223
Adrian, MI 49221
517-263-0771
www.merrillat.com
The largest manufacturer of cabinetry for the entire home in North America since 1985, with eleven manufacturing plants in the United States. Product lines include Organomics™, Amera, Merillat, and Woodward.

Plain & Fancy Custom Cabinetry
Route 501 & Oak Street
P.O. Box 519
Schaefferstown, PA 17088
800-447-9006
www.plainfancycabinetry.com
Plain & Fancy, a family-run company for thirty-one years, stands for quality workmanship at a surprisingly affordable price. Each cabinet is built using time-tested methods: mortise and tenon construction and dovetail drawers.

Poggenpohl U.S., Inc.
145 US Highway 46 West, Suite 200
Wayne, NJ 07470
973-812-8900
www.poggenpohl-usa.com
This world-renowned European kitchen and bath cabinet manufacturer produces and designs unique culinary areas in both contemporary and traditional design, with a large variety of front styles in wood, lacquer, laminate, veneer, aluminum, and stainless steel.

Portland Cement Association
5420 Old Orchard Road
Skokie, Illinois 60077-1083
847-966-6200
www.portcement.org
A trade association based in Skokie, Illinois, PCA conducts research, education, and public affairs work on behalf of its members – U.S. and Canadian cement companies.

Schrock Cabinets
One Master Brand Cabinets Dr.
Jasper, IN 47546
812-482-2527
www.aristokraft.com
Convenience inside, beauty outside, Schrock offers quality cabinetry with flexible storage and design options to create kitchens that balance fashion and function. Designed for the way we live, Schrock creates cabinetry solutions.

Simonton Windows
P.O. Box 1646
Parkersburg, WV 26102
800-542-9118
www.simonton.com
Since 1946, Simonton Windows has taken pride in delivering quality, energy efficient vinyl windows and patio doors. With a wide range of products available coast-to-coast, the company is committed to understanding your needs and exceeding your expectations.

Snaidero USA
20300 S. Vermont Ave., Suite 125
Los Angeles, CA 90502
310-516-8499
sales@snaidero-usa.com
www.snaidero-usa.com
Snaidero has pioneered luxury kitchen design for over half a century in Europe. Renowned for collaborations with elite designers such as Ferari stylist Pininfarina and famed Italian architects Lucci and Orlandini, it remains a contemporary luxury design trendsetter.

StarMark, Inc.
600 E. 48th St. N.
Sioux Falls, SD 57104
605-335-8600
www.StarMarkCabinetry.com
Fine StarMark cabinetry offers choices to let you express yourself with full creative freedom. Choose from a comprehensive selection of woods, finishes, accessories, fashion elements, and true custom options.

Style Solutions, Inc.
960 West Barre Road
Archbold, OH 43502
800-446-3040
www.stylesolutions.com
Manufacturer of over 4,000 quality urethane millwork products for the interior and exterior of homes, including window and door trim, moldings, louvers, balustrade systems, ceiling medallions, and wall niches.

Varenna Poliform
150 East 58th Street, 9th Floor
New York, NY 10155
877-827-3662
www.poliformUSA.com
Varenna kitchens offer creative freedom, with all the ingredients to create "living" space in the widest sense; ambiences that provide maximum functionality with the warmth and vitality of familiar kitchens.

Victoria Benatar Urban – Architect
220 E. 65th St. #15-B
New York, NY 10021
212-755-0525
www.e-arquitectura.com
This New York-based design firm develops interior design, architecture, digital, and urban design projects worldwide, especially in New York, Miami, and Caracas, Venezuela. Urban has taught at Columbia University and Parsons School of Design.

Viking Range Corporation
111 Front Street
Greenwood, MS 38930
662-455-1200
www.vikingrange.com
Viking Range Corporation offers a complete line of professional-style cooking, ventilation, kitchen cleanup, and refrigeration equipment. Each product represents the finest in heavy-duty, commercial-type construction, performance, and appearance.

Weather Shield Windows & Doors
PO Box 309
Medford, WI 54451
715-748-2100
www.weathershield.com
Premium manufacturer of custom made windows for the home, offering six

different product lines including windows and doors for high-end luxury homes, remodeling projects, and historic renovations.

Wellborn Cabinet, Inc.
38669 Highway 77
Ashland, AL 36251
256-354-7022
www.wellborncabinet.com
Wellborn Cabinet offers over a hundred different door styles, all hand-sanded, and hand finished in a choice of over fifty finishes. More than seven hundred accessory cabinets are available for the kitchen or for any room of the home.

Wood-Mode Inc.
One Second Street
Kreamer, PA 17833
800-635-7500
www.wood-mode.com
The company features a full line of custom, built-in cabinetry for every room of the home. Two basic construction options—framed and frameless—are available in more than ninety door styles and one hundred finishes, with a lifetime limited warranty.

YesterTec Design Company
PO Box 190
Center Valley, PA 18034
877-346-4976
www.yestertec.com
This company specializes in appliance-concealing cabinetry that resembles freestanding furniture, integrating function with the comfortable, timeless feel of furniture.

Yorktowne Cabinets
P.O. Box 231
Red Lion, PA 17356
717-244-4011
www.yorktowneinc.com
A member of the Elkay Cabinet Group, Yorktowne has been one of the nation's largest producers of stock and semi-custom cabinets for almost a century.

Great Kitchen Designs
A Visual Feast of Ideas and Resources
Tina Skinner

370 full-color pictures of hundreds of beautiful kitchens to help you create your own unique cooking/dining/entertaining environment. All the elements of beautiful kitchens—flooring, cabinetry, windows, walls, lighting, appliances, surrounds, backsplashes and more—are pictured and discussed. Includes a special chapter on the small kitchen, plus a resource guide listing designers and manufacturers. An invaluable resource for anyone planning to remodel an old kitchen or build a new one and a great reference book for kitchen design professionals.

Size: 8 1/2" x 11"	370 color photos	176 pp.
ISBN: 0-7643-1211-1	soft cover	$29.95

Big Book of Kitchen Design Ideas
Tina Skinner

Over 300 color photographs of kitchens including award-winning and fancy product ideas for manufacturers of cabinetry, countertops, windows, appliances, and floors. Contemporary, country, classic European, early American, and Art Deco kitchens and special needs for elderly and handicapped users are all identified. Designed for the do-it-yourselfer or as a bank of illustrations to share with a designer or contractor.

Size: 8 1/2" x 11"	321 color photos	144 pp.
ISBN: 0-7643-0672-3	soft cover	$24.95

20th Century Bathroom Design by Kohler
Tina Skinner

Take a chronological tour of bathrooms and watch as they evolved from converted closets to luxury centers for relaxation. More than 400 images are from advertising and designer rooms created for Kohler Co., including painted designs for toilets, sinks, matching tiles, and wooden vanities. Hundreds of early products are pictured to identify antique styles and a gallery of contemporary bathroom design has nearly 150 photos.

Size: 8 1/2" x 11"	401 color and B&W photos	176 pp.
ISBN: 0-7643-0614-6	soft cover	$29.95

Barn-Style Homes
Design Ideas for Timber Frame Houses
Tina Skinner and Tony Hanslin

A must-have for anyone who owns or wants to build a timber-frame house, or remodel a barn. Includes stunning images from 37 custom-built homes complete with floor plans. Furnishing and decorating ideas for great rooms, master bedrooms, cozy sitting rooms, elegant dining rooms, home offices, kitchens and baths, and lofty hideaways.

Size: 8 1/2" x 11"	275 color photos, 37 illus	192 pp.
Resource Guide		
ISBN: 0-7643-1319-3	hard cover	$39.95

Bright Ideas
Sunrooms & Conservatories
Tina Skinner

Interior and exterior photographs of sunrooms, conservatories, greenhouses, and great glass walls will help you select the right style for your architecture, as well as your lifestyle. Includes ideas for furnishing your indoor extension into the great outdoors, from formal dining areas to comfy family gathering spots, plus tub and pool rooms, patio rooms and indoor gardens, even kitchens and fanciful Florida rooms.

Size: 8 1/2" x 11"	189 photos	160 pp.
Resource Guide		
ISBN: 0-7643-1418-1	soft cover	$29.95

Lighting 2000
A Guide to the Best in Contemporary Lighting Design
Tina Skinner

More than 60 of today's top lighting designers showcased in over 350 color photos. Included are chandelier and ceiling fixtures, wall sconces, and table and floor lamps. The ultimate shoppers' guide for anyone hunting for the unique and special. Also includes an index of design studios and suggested retail prices for items shown. A must-have for professional interior designers, and an invaluable tool for any homeowner shopping for the best.

Size: 8 1/2" x 11"	342 color photos	112 pp.
Price Guide/Index		
ISBN: 0-7643-1156-5	soft cover	$19.95

All Decked Out...Redwood Decks
Ideas and Plans for Contemporary Outdoor Living
Tina Skinner

Over 200 color photographs of decks from around the country are presented with plans and ideas for overcoming slopes, incorporating trees, encircling spas, creating conversation pits, and enhancing gardens. Additions like stylized railings or varied floor patterns can suggest Japanese gardens or colonial elegance. A cut-out planner and hints to get started will help refocus life in the great outdoors.

Size: 8 1/2" x 11"		160 pp.
	212 color photos/31 illus.	
ISBN: 0-7643-0510-7	soft cover	$29.95

Pure Deck-adence
A Guide to Beautiful Decks
Tina Skinner

Here is a fantasy collection of real-life deck photos from all over the United States. This pictorial essay explores America's fascination with outdoor living, from barbecue-centered constructions to the new immersion in hot tub culture. More than 240 full-color photographs provide a rich resource of ideas for those who dream of expanding their homes, and their horizons, with wood decks.

Size: 8 1/2" x 11"	246 color photos	160 pp.
ISBN: 0-7643-0445-3	hard cover	$29.95

Outdoor Wood Works
With Complete Plans for Ten Projects
Tina Skinner

A collection of ideas for improving the environment around the house. Hundreds of ideas are presented in full-color photographs. Permanent outdoor fixtures like benches and gazebos make the environs more comfortable, while flower boxes, retaining walls, and other accents add beauty. Ten complete project plans, from a simple screen around a utility box to an outdoor storage shed, are included.

Size: 8 1/2" x 11"	146 color photos	160 pp.
ISBN: 0-7643-0446-1	hard cover	$19.95

Schiffer books may be ordered from your local bookstore, or they may be ordered directly from the publisher by writing to:
Schiffer Publishing, Ltd.
4880 Lower Valley Rd
Atglen PA 19310
(610) 593-1777; Fax (610) 593-2002
E-mail: schifferbk@aol.com
Please visit our website catalog at *www.schifferbooks.com* or write for a free catalog. Please include $3.95 for shipping and handling for the first two books and 50¢ for each additional book. Free shipping for orders of $100 or more.
Printed in China

MORE SCHIFFER TITLES

WWW.SCHIFFERBOOKS.COM

Take a tour of more than 200 kitchens and gather ideas for your own culinary center. Nearly 300 beautiful color images help you choose cabinet door styles, wood finishes, floor textures, and colors to suit your tastes. Special emphasis is placed on the small to mid-size kitchen, with great examples of storage solutions and space enhancing designs. This is a virtual showroom for the professional designer or remodeler who wants to hash through ideas with clients, and a great way for homeowners to express the tastes. Here's the first step toward a showplace kitchen: your sticky tabs out and start marking the elements that would like to see in your home.

US $24.95

9 780764 315107   52495

ISBN: 0-7643-1510-2

$3.99

548090
a129-
033-P